RETURN BY MINOR ROAD

'Through poems of meticulous clarity and precision, Williamson charts the lives and landscapes of a tragedy and its aftermath. These are poems which honestly and respectfully explore the two worlds of humanity: the world we inhabit, its towns, fields and rivers; and, equally importantly, the emotional and spiritual context – the world which inhabits us. What binds the two together? In this powerful and moving collection, it is surely love.' – JOHN GLENDAY

'A subtle, moving collection that embraces and explores the landscape cut into the heart. With profound moments and a cumulative power, the collection encapsulates how place and the past are a continuing emotional reality.' – ESTHER MORGAN

'Williamson has achieved an impressively finely-tuned response to the Dunblane massacre. Adventurous, intriguing, with a sense of being compelled to return, of the sequence taking its own quiet path. A very valuable book indeed.' – MONIZA ALVI

'*Return by Minor Road* is a wonder. Almost unbearably moving at times, these poems evoke the elemental nature of memory, our animal striving for survival, and the horror that human beings so often inflict upon each other. In three sections, the haunting of trauma, the returning in memory, and the return in actuality to honour the dead, Williamson reminds us that our most sacred responsibility is to remember.' – DAN O'BRIEN

Born in Norfolk in 1971, **Heidi Williamson** has lived in central Scotland, Brussels and Salisbury. She now lives in Wymondham, Norfolk. She is an Advisory Fellow for the Royal Literary Fund, and was Royal Literary Fund Fellow at the University of East Anglia from 2018 to 2020. From 2011 to 2014, she was writer-in-residence at the John Jarrold Printing Museum in Norwich and in 2008-09 was poet-in-residence at the London Science Museum's Dana Centre. In 2008 she received an Arts Council award to complete her first collection, *Electric Shadow* (Bloodaxe Books, 2011), a Poetry Book Society Recommendation, which was shortlisted for the Seamus Heaney Centre for Poetry Prize. *The Print Museum* (Bloodaxe Books, 2016) won the Poetry Category and the Book by the Cover award in the 2016 East Anglian Book Awards. Her third collection, *Return by Minor Road*, was published by Bloodaxe Books in 2020.

Her work has been used to inspire poetry and science discussions in schools and adult creative writing groups, and has featured in NHS waiting rooms, cafés, and at festivals. Poems have been translated into Polish, Turkish, Romanian and German. She works with poets worldwide by Skype as a poetry surgeon for The Poetry Society, teaches for The Poetry School, and mentors poets through The Writing Coach, National Centre for Writing and The Poetry School. For more information, see her website www.heidiwilliamsonpoet.com

HEIDI WILLIAMSON

Return by
Minor Road

BLOODAXE BOOKS

ISBN: 978 1 78037 522 9

First published 2020 by
Bloodaxe Books Ltd,
Eastburn,
South Park,
Hexham,
Northumberland NE46 1BS.

www.bloodaxebooks.com
For further information about Bloodaxe titles
please visit our website and join our mailing list
or write to the above address for a catalogue

Supported using public funding by
**ARTS COUNCIL
ENGLAND**

Cover design: Neil Astley & Pamela Robertson-Pearce.

Printed in Great Britain by Bell & Bain Limited, Glasgow, Scotland, on
acid-free paper sourced from mills with FSC chain of custody certification.

In remembrance:
Dunblane, 13 March 1996

CONTENTS

III The wild rain

our fleeting lives do not simply 'happen'
and vanish – they *take place*

JANE HIRSHFIELD

1 What the river leaves behind

13 March 2018

The city, though it has only a village population, is well worth
visiting… It has a mineral spring, to which many visitors resort
during the summer months. Tannahill's beautiful song of 'Jessie,
the flower of Dunblane' has given it popularity. The Allan runs
through the village. A beautiful foot road by the river… runs
between Dunblane and Bridge of Allan.

Bradshaw's handbook for tourists (London: Adams, 1858)

On the anniversary of the tragedy, survivors and relatives of
victims from Dunblane posted a video of support to students
affected by the high school shooting in Parkland, Florida.

Dunblane Stands with Parkland, 13 March 2018
[www.youtube.com/watch?v=6-nEzMbfyNk]

The wall

Nights you call out, I pad
the hallway to your duvet flung wide,
your leg dangling down, tender and crooked,
still warm, your small palm cooling on the wall.

Your soft toys shift and slide as I cover you.
My mind slides towards small absent ones
I cared for in passing. Long ago, I glanced into
the room of a girl who turned from the wall in sleep.

Edging between the wall and the soft anchorage
of my bed, I turn my bedspread back; lay hands
along its length – see how awkwardly
it rucks, how hard it is to settle.

In a school room, the woodcutter

had come for the children

Every wolf that he could muster

herded them into the darkened forest

they tried to be small   as birds, quieter

one feather   pressed to their beaks

The woodcutter

called to them   with his shiny
voice

The children lay their heads

beneath their wings and waited

An erasure of 'Woodcutter', Heidi Williamson (*Electric Shadow*, 2011)

Thrawn

adj. Chiefly Scottish
1. Crooked, twisted, misshapen.
2. Stubborn, persistent.

In sleep, my eyelids fail to close
completely. Two small moons
shiver below unsettled lashes.

It's then I go back to the river.
Nut-brown in spate, it hoards soil
from the slopes, grates branches

on stone, bears fallen trees
full-across. The tow-back
from the weir is brawny.

Tonight, the river offshoots
– it streams thrawn
beneath the high street.

Some houses are lifted,
some begin to blacken
as the water-level reaches

into each cell of stone.
Surfaces peel, float
away from themselves.

A skeleton could deflect
the water with its body,
create an arch

so the water laps and falls,
a hollow that admits
the river and directs it.

Then my eyelids will shutter
completely. The full moons beneath
will witness themselves closed.

Cormorant

The cormorant inside my head
peers at the one in my heart.
It shakes its beak,
gestures with its wings
that it's time to open, to fly.

The cormorant inside my heart
calls back: *Run*, but a cormorant
can't run. *Hide*, it calls,
but such a bird can't hide.
Fight. It flexes its wings wide.

Run-hide-fight is an active shooter drill US schoolchildren practise
from the age of five.

Weir

The path is still artificially lit; the darkness
just now outfalling. The river's spate outstays
last night's downpour, churning itself over
like the mind on a worry. Debris wavers on
the weir or is thrashed on an unplanned course.

A cormorant stretches out its wings on the bluff
in the early morning. Making its cross on the crag,
it claims survival space among the colony.
Unlike other water birds, its flight feathers let
the water enter: it must open out to recompose.

At the whim of the weather, the water will drop;
the paths in the distance become merely dark
with the aftermath. The river will outlast this rush
but not mourn it. The cormorant will not grieve
for what it never knew to be its difference.

Loch Occasional

The things I do not want to write about
become the things I write about.

EIMEAR McBRIDE

Mid-winter or spring, sometimes
the Balvaig floods Balquhidder Glen;
gives rise to a short-lived body.

This uncommon water hosts
fresh species that feed and breed there:
sculpin, caddisflies, pearl mussels.

The flood may recede
as rapidly as it arrived. Landslides
may follow. This too, opens up

the canopies, the strata of soil.
Buried nutrients, seeds,
live plant matter is scattered.

Silt beds down. The surface
tension levels. The landscape
is transformed again.

Sudden creatures enrich the area
or deplete it. Fragments enter
the disturbed ground. Waken.

*

Spring or mid-winter, at other times
too, the silt of what happened rises
and drops with the level of days.

Sometimes it covers all daily tasks
with an oily sheen that dimples
when pressed, then releases

the surface tension, the water's skin.
Forced out to the edges of itself,
all becomes water.

It may recede, but the days
are not transformed. The days
are delayed, waiting for the water

to come back, to scatter
live matter back in its place.
The occasional endures.

What the river leaves behind

Inhale and you will miss it. The breath of water
rising above the river, following it towards sunset.
As the river's breath rises, you may find yours

shortens, worries at your lungs.
You may stand on its banks some days and resist
the temptation to walk in up to your chest.

What the river leaves behind
doesn't matter to time or the river.
What the river leaves behind is all breaths.

It's twenty-two years ago and it's today

You wake at five with our son, leave me to pretend to sleep. Our two cats settle on my legs. We eat breakfast separately. I lose myself in the bath. You clean. Toilets. Bathroom. Hoover. Dust. We seldom dust. You disinfect the kitchen sink. I iron our small crumpled things. Our son moans about the wind interfering with playing football. We think. We can't think. We stare at the garden. Pretend to watch the birds. The cat wails to go out. We let it. It dashes back with the wind in its tail. It cries to go back out again. We are quiet. We are kind. We respect. We don't read the papers. We leave our phones off. We go out for a simple lunch. Our son eats cake. Is allowed a Coke. We shop for Sunday's chicken. We play Pokémon at the kitchen table. I witness his yo-yo tricks. We watch CBBC for a while. Eventually I write. Small hard coughs on the page. I am so slow at this. We eat baked sweet potatoes with cheese and beans. Bonfire food. We keep close. We keep our thoughts to ourselves. We drink wine. Not too much. Plan to go to bed early. We know neither of us will sleep. We put tea lights on the table. Neither of us says why. We save shouting for the next day.

Bracklinn Falls

What is buried beneath these falls
chafes against the backflow of water
that weathers these mudstone ledges.

The water's own reflection froths
back at it madly. It chases itself
away – again and again

over light-grey-brown
oblong stones, solid as doors –
the river forceful as a key.

Watching the past in the waters of Loch Earn

Not water sprites, but past selves
guttering beneath the surface of the loch.

They shoal towards me.
The ripples of their hair

invite and warn;
their voices incoherent to me now.

By day, I know them by their movements
as they mass here, sealed below.

At night, I know them
by disruptions in the darkness.

I never stoop to reach
down into the cold; never trouble

their interweaving
translucent bones.

I know them though:
know their routes, know their borders.

One by one, more of them
will drift here in future.

What will it take for them
to let in the thrum of the wind,

let in the smoothness of stones,
let in the weight of the rain?

The rain in the night

The past is falling on the house
lightly, insistently
with its own unnameable scent.

I can't tell when the first mist
of it began to drift down,
lifting itself gently – down.

It wasn't there, then it was
all around the house,
moving across the roof
with a patterning I couldn't recognise.

In a way there wasn't much of it,
but such slivers
bear down over time.

The roof gradually succumbs
to a fresh deepening colour.
The night insects bed down
out of the spattering.
The wisteria darkens,
drops petals.

Even a light scattering
leaves its mark in the morning,
even if the surface dries.

The soft past of rain
has shaken itself on the house.
The house – defenceless
against its lightness.

Fugitive dust

Child in the doorway who appears
and disappears around the edge
of my open book, how do you find me?

The landing light stutters in your presence,
the pale carpet shifts and shapes
around your boneless toes.

Child in the doorway who appears
each evening without footsteps,
I can hear you – breathing.

Still as a frame, you hold
yourself up softly.
Your clothes resist sight.

Child in the doorway who appears
a creature or chrysalis
of fugitive dust – your presence

fills my mouth with the tang of blood;
I daren't move or swallow
for fear you might withdraw.

Child in the doorway who appears
when the scent of wood-smoke drifts
onto the duvet, cautious as mist,
will you never step forwards?

Lepus timidus

So soft
is the fur

of the currently –

LOUISE MATHIAS, 'Larrea'

Tundra hare, turned
white before the snows,
your new hide exposes
tender flesh to undue clarity.

Your slender weight
sows narrow pathways
of terror management
between nightfall and daybreak

as you run uphill on the scree,
screaming the eagle away.
Territories of nibbled bilberries
and heather betray you.

Still your fur shivers,
awaiting the winter at its height
to match your pelt's maturity.
Winter might just strip us bare.

Tharn

Dead terror stills:

the hare engraves itself
on the air, the field;

the frosted field
stiffens its silence;
the bracken backs into itself;

regardless, light persists.

Tharn: fixed in fear

Hare

What if the dangerous thing actually happens
and you're elsewhere, looking away – at a hare
on the grass in the grounds of the offices.
You're twirling the phone cord and listening,
bored, to an adviser advise you on what's wrong
with the mortgage application that shouldn't be wrong
because you should know that the *Homeowner 3*
is the wrong form for the wrong customer,
and he's tired of doing your job for you.
And the hare is as still as an eye.
And the hare begins to flicker
like a screen running out of power
and the hare against the grass becomes flat
as a moment, like any terror
you can fall through – into the past.

II Cold spring

13 March 1996

[A gunman], having entered the school, shot Mrs Gwen Mayor and 16 members of her class and inflicted gunshot wounds on 10 other pupils and three other members of the teaching staff…

…the idea that anyone might enter school premises to commit assault 'never crossed our minds'. However…intruders would now require to be considered.

THE CULLEN INQUIRY

Never such innocence again.

PHILIP LARKIN, 'MCMXIV'

From

From the hallway you can see into every corner of our small flat.
From the kitchen window: the rose garden, golf course, the Trossachs.
From the bath you can see Glen Road's sky and sky framed.
From tomorrow all this will be different.

Scottish spring

Here, now, it's cold and snowdrops
have not yet ceded to daffodils.

Elsewhere, it's warming, dimmer;
already the snowdrops are dropping.

Now is the time when the world
is blown open.

Monochrome

The last time I saw you,
really saw you, was in the office
that day when the announcements
started to come, but no one
understood yet what had happened.
You stood up, sharply pushed back
your chair so it straggled across
the passageway. Your tidy desk
lay exposed to dust that would build
between stacked papers.
As you walked away, you were pale,
your face – open.

*

I saw you again
at the funeral
but couldn't see you
really, couldn't
see anything, not
because of the tears
but the blankness
my eyes and brain held,
and my heart: it's true
that the heart
halts as it hurts on.

*

I read you in the papers,
friend: I see you
and I read you and I wish
to hold your monochrome hand
as it rests across that small child's head.

Cold spring

I

a day like

habit   unbroken

*

our house on the hill

      the pheasant, the Siamese, the ducks

breezeblocks painted over

      the cupboard from hell – coat rack, junk store, circular
      window

*

ice stumbling from inside the windowpanes
the path loch-still

*

watching the birds above
the clouds the wind
all

*

the bridge
the river

*

flexitime clock-in mugs cups coffee-run coats steaming
eyes nose streaming folders out earphones on files notes
pen switch screen welcome detail

*

manager

                            says

        incident

        *

no one moment   with another

frozen   unaware

        *

a falling   order unfurled

of meaning   shut down

shared out   astray

happening to

unexpected unprepared nothing to prevent

      *

those moments   when the children you know,

you think, are   still

        there is none
        there is none

a hair's breadth
a single hair on their

no

      *

incoherent bystander

      *

mid-day home

    whole country calling   black words

strung between   mobile masts

    *

the name of our place

repeated until

    *

you want to jolt awake
you want

    *

all falls
through
against
around
beyond

all falls   broken

    *

there is a crying that is bone

Calls

You're there! the voice says,
then halts.

What else to say?
Yes, we're here.

I nod. I carry on nodding –
at the white plastic handset,

the slab of the base,
the cord twisting away

through the wires to everywhere else.
What else to say?

We're here, where the news is.
Where the day won't stop.

Where the phone keeps ringing
late into the evening.

Each time, the same redundant speech.
The same necessary reaching.

We couldn't get through.
I cup the earpiece against my skull,

the mouthpiece against my cheek.
It warms with contact.

I know. I say eventually.
And it means all it means.

After

'...we're all living in after'

MONIZA ALVI

We go to the pub we always go to.
Blair the barman is there, the locals
and the Sky News reporters
asking everyone to comment.

We hesitate at the door,
not because we don't want to talk,
though we don't – only
pausing, outside a few moments.

Blair beckons us over,
serves us and I stretch
my hand over his an instant
longer paying. He lets it stay,
nods, then looks away
and we find our quiet table.

Describe

It was   larger

unable

                              sacrifice

a village, a ruin

An erasure of 'Let Us Describe', Gertrude Stein.

Flowers

Work buses keep to their routes
but slow as we pass the flowers
fading field-high on the pavement.
Everyone's come far.

And

And the postman. And the florist. And the dentist. And the bus driver. And the sports coach. And the music tutor. And the friends. And the cousins. And the babysitter. And the crèche. And the train driver. And the road sweeper. And the bin men. And the window cleaner. And the windscreen replacement team. And the boiler repair man. And the carpet fitter. And the pizza delivery. And the neighbours. And the street. And the street across. And the town. And the county. And the island. And the continent. And the planet. And in space. And the stars. And the hairdresser. And the doctor. And the nurse. And the surgeon. And the paramedic. And the toyshop. And the sweet shop. And the cinema. And the newsagents. And the café. And the bar. And the pub. And the park. And the river. And the bridge. And the soil. And the wind. And the sunshine. And the rain. And the flowers. And the buildings. And the motorways. And the petrol station. And the supermarket. And the church. And the cathedral. And the library. And the roundabout. And the flags. And the bunting. And the pie shop. And the bakery. And the museum. And the walks. And the pathways. And the berries. And the birds. And the pets. And the vets. And the garage. And the cleaners. And the kitchen fitter. And the co-workers. And the corporation. And the stock market. And the royals. And the politicians. And the laws. And the procedures. And the neurons. And the possibilities. And the eventualities. And the next time. And the grandparents. And the teacher. And the classmates. And the siblings. And the parents. And the children. And.

Dumyat

Some days we cried ourselves out,
packed our coats and climbed
the soggy rock to its small summit.

There was something about stepping
one by one, beside each other
without speaking, without the need.

At the summit we kept numb vigil
for what we couldn't say.
We descended in mist,

our blurry outlines mottling
together. On spring days
now, when cold tips the hills

I can still see its cairn and trig point,
that chopped obelisk at its peak,
distant sheep folds, memorials of snow.

Balquhidder

After the bumpy, miles-long track, we stored
ourselves in a far cottage beyond water.
Small dogs visited us and scurried
something solemn out the door with them.
Thin place, where heaven and the afterlife
lie close to the surface of the day.
I bathed and slept and cried; you walked.
We were colder than we'd ever been,
despite the fire. Even when I watched
smoke chugging slowly from our own
chimney that day, I couldn't connect.
Were we smoke, were we cold, were we left?

Aubade

our bike leathers sag against the banister
where yesterday we surrendered them
having chased the light from the roads

Sheriffmuir

The bracken moults fine hairs;
browning with the heat,
it crackles as we brush past.

In the warm autumnal air
we scan for wildlife:
tundra hares may come this low.

Picking through the undergrowth
we scatter something, breaking
through and out into the light

we came to pause in. Too long
enclosed in small rooms
dusty with books and chores,

we stride the layered moor
on towards the Ochil Hills,
which clear us of ourselves.

Cold spring

II

what has been this day
what has been

    *

the body remembers

    *

human resources counsellors trained conference rooms warm
tea dirtied carpets how do you feel? what would you want to
say?

    *

newness   brings grief

the living need

    *

scanning the day

the years after

      *

shock   resets

*

go back   move

on
        move

      *

work, carrying

time is enough
               no

      *

     where is your rage

      *

new news

*

every name is the name

                        of someone who is

there

        *

days around us

earth

cautioning us

spaces to be

        *

spring never far away

Elegy

Victoria Clydesdale   Emma Crozier

Melissa Currie   Charlotte Dunn   Kevin Hasell

Ross Irvine   David Kerr   Mhairi MacBeath

Gwen Mayor   Brett McKinnon

Abigail McLennan   Emily Morton

Sophie North   John Petrie   Joanna Ross

Hannah Scott   Megan Turner

Snowdrop

Every year they break through
hard ground, their tiny selves
weighed down with sunlight.

The Snowdrop Campaign after the Dunblane tragedy led to the
UK introducing some of the world's strictest gun-ownership laws.

III   The wild rain

1996 –

The community was in a state of sadness, shock and disbelief.
People felt stunned, unable to take in the enormity of the horrific
tragedy at our school. I remember a sense of being cold for days
with a heavy feeling of despair deep inside. I recall thinking that
if I feel like this, it must be unbearable for the families who had
lost children and the others whose children were injured. There
were also the many people who had tried to help and witnessed
scenes too unbearable to describe. Compared to these people
I was unaffected, yet I did feel deeply affected. I know many
others who felt the same.

NORA GILFILLAN
The Dunblane Centre: The Gift That Keeps Growing
(Jamieson and Munro, 2014)

When we were stone

We were fine-grained, sedimentary.
Our bedding planes were fissile.

We slept at the bottom of a river;
when it dried we basked,

when it froze we waited.
The stars were further

when we saw them through water.
The river's bed near-buried us.

Its silt suppressed
or collided against us.

Over the years how worn we grew.
So many elements fused between.

The fish eyed us with suspicion.
And when we drained in the sun

dragonflies alighted on us
as if we would always be there.

Culvert

My unassuming heart
became a valley
amassing waters and debris

— a vehicle for rain
dashing down the sides
in emergency free-fall.

It isn't true to say
that the valley gloved the heart,
it was the heart,

rent in the same way
a clearing is made
by great and incremental

incidents. Partly
the valley remains
visible beneath land

that's been cleared
for new lives and families
— its pulse ebbs in culverts

below neat estates,
a furtive love trickling
deeper and deeper.

With a rootless lily held in front of him

No one ever told me that grief felt so like fear

C.S. LEWIS, *A Grief Observed*

Like someone stepping slowly ahead
of an old-fashioned car, or the person tasked
with carrying the country's Olympic flame,
he must hold the lily as he walks, sits, speaks, listens.

He holds it low, his arms relaxed,
accustomed to its movement.
The long stem reaches to his breastbone.
The lily's pale skull barely moves as he moves.
Open and upright, the petals are stiff and fragile.
The yellowy-orange stamen is a risk.
Everyone knows it could stain you.
With each breath he inhales its scent,
each exhalation ghost-feeds it.

Each person he meets will ask
or choose deliberately not to ask.
Each person sees the lily first,
then perhaps the man.

Some wonder what the lily does
when he sleeps. Or what happens
when this stalk, as it surely must,
fades and withers. Some suspect him
of slyly replacing it to freshen its bloom.
Each person considers touching the petals.

There are those who think it distasteful
to bring the lily out into the open.
To them it's like a begging bowl.

In many ways his lily is no different
to any lily of theirs. Though they'd never
say it aloud, a few have a terrible doubt
that he somehow deserves his.

Sometimes he allows his focus to shift
through its arch-backed petals.
Sometimes he forgets he still holds it.

Tonight my heart is open so hard it could shatter

There is enough of the air to go round but I sip it slimly in
and out, in and out like a small fish flapping out of water.

Even the worms in the ground hear the rain better
than I do. Over the whine of the TV, the cars noising by,

it's so hard to hear the heart thinking. But here,
now – how thought breaks into it,
                                    on and on.

Every day

I

I walk our son all the way to his classroom door.
He thinks this is his idea.

II

I text you to say we arrived safely.
I text you to say I collected him.

III

I wait guiltily
outside locked gates.

IV

The first day there is an ambulance
outside the care home next to our son's school
my feet start running towards the gate. I can't stop them.

V

Our son joins Gym Club. He joins Cubs.
He wants a combat paintball birthday party.

VI

On World Book Day, even his costume
for Young Sherlock comes with a pistol.

VII

We try to act normal about these things.

Allan Water bridge

Prickly moss ridges
between her fingers
as she presses her palms
down on the edge.

Slivers of dark mortar
grate against her skin.
She watches the water below
ring against the abutments.

When she raises both palms
gently from the surface
of the crumbling brickwork,
the bridge begins to hover

one inch above the water,
then begins to move
effortlessly forwards.

The bridge slides
alongside and past
the mill, the houses,
glides by soft green
fields of sheep.

The woman and the bridge
drift along the surface
of the river like this
for as long as she looks
deep into the water.
Dark fish weave beneath.

When she turns her gaze
away, the bridge silently
moors. She knows this place.

Carefully placing her palms
back down on the brickwork,
she rouses herself.

Leaving the bridge, she takes
the low route to the cottage
that is no longer there.

Facing north

Water-rills across wet tarmac
flick light back
even under thunderclouds.

The run of thickets breaks
and the water-light draws
motes across the forest air.

Spores are at work here.
The scent of stones.
Water unearthed.

These small movements
towards the bracken
are to be reckoned with.

Disappearance at six o'clock

It is the going underground that preserves the body

STEPHANIE BOLSTER,
'Portrait of Alice with Persephone'

Alice, it's time to step out
of your dream now,

time to come up for air;
rest on the bank like a coin on snow.

The sky's in the river,
blue and white as an apron;

clouds in the water
like drowned breaths.

The water is soundless:
even your echo has gone.

In the cold blue light
there's a hole full of girl.

The river is not following anywhere.
Come, Alice, it's time to go home.

Return by minor road

can you say that a man is lost just because
you cannot distinguish him from the background.

COLE SWENSEN,
'Chaïm Soutine: The Errant Road, 1939'

We go back quietly, in surprising sunshine.
The warmth opens us, as our child sweats
into the Scottish air, declaring the hill
too long; a mountain. He says the light
tastes different here. It nestles on our tongues.
Dark pillars of firs line the driveway
down to our old home. The once-green
cottage window-frames are grey,
making the house look shabbier
or more in keeping with the usual weather.
We visit the current tenants. Drink tea.
Make small talk. After, our son lopes ahead
back down to the memorial bear and fox,
rests his wrists on their cool marble;
a good way to recalibrate the body.
Inside the cathedral, the air channels
towards the altar. A rabbit, a camel, all manner
of creatures perch at the end of pews
in clean-cut wood the colour of hazelnuts.
On the graveyard wall, an emptied can
of Tennent's Super is haloed by sunlight.
In the hotel, we play a racing game
brought down from the bookshelves.
He gallops his horses forwards, forwards.

Dunblane

Walking the hill to our old flat,
the pubs and benches we used to visit
accumulate behind us.

The Golf Club rests greenly in its aisle.
The old new Tesco seems emptier now.

We discover play parks, museums,
heritage sites, that as students
we never deigned to find.

We watch the future
we dare not presume

run ahead towards
the climbing frames,
the swirled slide

that delivers him
lightly onto the earth.

The weight of news

I had lost not only a place but the past that goes with it, the clues from which to construct a present self.

EAVAN BOLAND, *Object Lessons*

Until I walked this road again, I would have sworn
    it was steeper. That the houses
were set back more deeply behind walls.

I thought there was more foliage, more cover.
    Perhaps the trees have grown, as I have not:
new leaves extending out of reach.

My body recalls slowly hiking
    this hill, backpack brimming
with shopping, heading home.

I reach the small crossroads of the drive.
    Birds, like debris, rise from the branches.
Blue-grey clouds mark the mid-morning sky.

Years ago, news arrived abruptly here.
    It lingers, inexplicable
in the presence of everything I see.

If I close my eyes, I can make this place again
    the small silent carousel
of landscapes and faces I roll out in times of need.

Still for a moment, I imagine it back.
    The casual beauty returns to the pavement.
Moss fuzzes the stone lines, greening their grey.

I open my eyes and step intently ahead
    in and out of the shadows;
letting the past back in, just as it was.

Historical markers

These gold-edged squares of interest and importance
set in the sides of buildings, the bridge – these plaques
are solid as teeth, surprising, in crumbling stone.

In what seems like a moment, they become odd as a house
seen from the garden first thing, when the mist clears and a window
hosts a disembodied torso turning on taps and boiling a kettle.

The chinks of cups, clicks of appliances and native bark
of a winter cough surprise the grass and its inhabitants:
the gold-edged eye of a blackbird commemorates this.

Like a blackbird, I like to sing after rain.
Like a blackbird, there is no sign I can add to my body
to state its past more accurately than my body.

Wet morning in the cathedral square

Dull steadiness of rain,
unnoticed as light.

Dye rises on the hem of each coat.
Leather darkness spreads.

Click of umbrellas hoisted,
wet hands on steel stems.

A child, umbrella-less, hands deep in pockets.
Each flavour of rain on the face.

In the courtyard, umbrellas tip
towards one another in speech.

On the pavement, a silver coin
gilded with rain shimmer.

Reliability of rain.
Durability of rain.

A language learned abroad

I also left a skin there

LOUISE GLÜCK, 'Cottonmouth Country'

Let the language of this land soften
into your being. Counter its shifting lilt

with a tilt of your own making.
You can love what is not understood.

In this place, they say: *Is that you?*
Are you away but?

The language here leaves you
drookit – soaked to the skin.

Though you can never catch up
what you say with what you mean

there are words for child and flight
you can take in and wean.

The trees of the Trossachs

The trees of the Trossachs and golf course,
framed by the kitchen window and garden,
come back to me now in silence.

In photographs, they interleave the years.
Now, they are as they were then:
they green and golden, wave and wane.

Birds have come and gone in them. Nests. Storms.
Clouds top them with intricate patterning.
The wind carries around the world and comes back.

Self

What are you doing here?

I don't know

What do you hope to achieve?

I don't know

How can you make words out of this?

I don't know

What if you bring more darkness?

I don't know

What are you guilty of?

I don't know

What are you ashamed of?

I don't know

What are you afraid of?

I don't know

Where are you heading with this?

I don't know

What can you tell your child?

I don't know

Why can't you say it?

I don't know

Why don't you know?

I don't know

Smoke

This time of year smoke renews
   – from bonfires in unseen gardens,
it flows grey-green across boundaries.

My son is green in his knowledge,
   his uniform green, his love
green-grey as unboundaried smoke.

This time of year his growth renews
   just as autumn is throwing out hers
– done with spring, summer,

done with holding up
   all those leaves, done
holding on to each tiny seed.

Smoke needn't be a warning,
   it can be an invitation –
the homestead is within your scent.

The hero in this poem
   throws invisible smoke bombs
to exit a room mysteriously.

From the school gates I spy him
   on the open field
– *pouf*, he's gone.

Dust, at intervals

The air is not nothing.
    It has a weight
        and livingness.

    In a narrow shaft of lamplight
        the eye of the dust
            holds against air.

Each brightness looks white,
    but gel-like translucent creatures
        ride the light:

    skin flakes, mites, cat dander,
        soil, particulate matter,
            rock sludge, Saharan sand.

    Tiny pale birds
        as they scatter to the ground,
            flock, vie for the centre, lift.

The wild rain

What waters our bodies have received
– each filament of rain
coursing the length of our skin
lies undiscovered now at this dark hour.

In here, the night is quiet and cool. Outside,
the wild rain courts the grass: even in the dark
I feel its greening – the glossed grass smooth as keratin
anchoring, protecting the dust of us.

I lean against the solidity of your clement body
soft with sleep, lean in to you. On your arm, your hand,
each tiny hair responds to my disclosing touch.
The territory of your body grounds me, strands me.

The grass has craved this all day:
the phantom rain fell too lightly to reach land,
the heavy sun striking out
droplets as they formed.

Above all, my uncontrollable heart
coils wild as the wild rain outside
springing right back up again
from the earth where it belongs.

Winter river

Though it looks unrivered,
this is not a riverless place.

In blizzard, the water is silenced.
Flakes swallow the river whole

– rock, boulder, bank grow into absences.
Ice freezes and refreezes into sediment.

The storm settles for so many days,
then the river is first to break free.

In a slow unwrapping,
the snow begins to loosen, crumble

like foam. The river begins to sprout.
Dull steel boulders edge out again.

No spring is needed – no green shoots.
The cry of a small bird will do it.

Whatever it takes, the river keeps going.
The river knows the way beneath the snows.

Place

When we left, we left it all:
the hazel, the spruce, the Scots pine, the aspen.

When we left we took it all:
the skyscapes and treescapes framing each season.

When we left, we left it all:
the bracken, the cabins, the pathways of water.

When we left we took it all:
the hollows, chill soil, ice-air and snowfall.

When we left, we left it all:
angular boulders with ashy thin grasses.

When we left we took it all:
scent of just-rained-on expanding the stonework.

When we left, we left it all:
pine martens, red deer, herons and osprey.

When we left we took it all:
broadening rain-clouds blending with hillsides.

When we left, we left it all:
short-lived supple islands of shingle.

When we left we took it all:
the bend in the loch we can't see beyond.

ACKNOWLEDGEMENTS

Acknowledgements are due to the editors of the following magazines where some of these poems first appeared: *Abstract: Contemporary Expressions* (New York), *Empty Mirror* (Washington), *London Grip*, *Manchester Review*, *Marble*, *MONK*, *New Welsh Review*, *One* (Jacar Press), *Poetry Spotlight*, *South Bank Poetry*, *Strix*, *SWWIM Every Day* (Miami), *Tentacular*, *The Curlew*, *The Fenland Reed*, *The High Window*, *The Lampeter Review*, *The Moth*, *The North*, *The Reader*, *Whale Road Review* (San Diego).

'Disappearance at six o'clock' was commissioned for *Alice/Ekphrasis at the British Library*, ed. Gillespie, Morley, Smith (Joy Lane Publishing, 2016). 'Weir' appeared under a different title in *Land of Three Rivers: the poetry of North-East England*, ed. Neil Astley (Bloodaxe Books, 2017).

'With a rootless lily held in front of him' was shortlisted for the Bridport Prize 2019. 'A language learned abroad' was shortlisted for the Live Canon poetry competition 2018 and included in the Live Canon Poetry Anthology 2018.

The collection's epigraph is from *Nine Gates: Entering the Mind of Poetry* by Jane Hirshfield (HarperCollins, 1998). 'Fugitive dust' takes its title from a line in 'understory' by Craig Santos Perez. 'Cold spring' includes a quote from Gerard Manley Hopkins' 'No worst there is none, pitched past pitch of grief'. 'Wet morning in the cathedral square' is after Archibald David Reid's painting 'A wet morning in Dunblane cathedral square'. Thanks to the staff at Dunblane Museum, especially Lynda Lord.

Love and thanks to Gary Williamson, Alex Williamson, Sue Burge, Julia Webb, Moniza Alvi, Esther Morgan, John Glenday, Richard Lambert, Jo Guthrie, Laura Scott, Kathryn Simmonds, Keiron Pim, Bex Barrow, Bridget Beauchamp, Clare Jarrett, Sally Paramour, Nina Robertson, David Tait, Seán Hewitt, Sean O'Brien, Sarah Byrne, and the Norwich Stanza group.